I0148891

TAKE THE GLOVES OFF
My Journey

Dr. Deveonne Cooke

WISEWORD Publishing, LLC
USA

WISEWORD Publishing, LLC

USA

Copyright © 2011 Deveonne Cooke, PsyD, LICDC

All rights reserved.

No part of this book may be reproduced, stored in a retrieval system, or transmitted in any form or by any means—electronic, mechanical, photocopying, recording, or otherwise—without the prior written permission of the publisher and copyright owner.

Additional copyright information is contained in the back matter of this book.

ISBN: 978-0-9839185-2-3

3rd Printing

Published by WISEWORD Publishing, LLC
Columbus, Ohio
For Worldwide Distribution

Printed in the United States of America

Contents

This Book

Is

Dedicated to the memory of my loving parents

Alfred and Bernice
Married 44 years

Many waters cannot quench love, neither can the floods drown it: if a man would give all the substance of his house for love, it would utterly be condemned. Song of Solomon 8:7

iii

Acknowledgements

Heavenly Father, your Son, Jesus and Holy Spirit, I love you with my whole being . . . thank you for life, unconditional love, my gifts, your example and guidance.

To my parents for a sure foundation of Godly values, love, nurturing and family solidarity;

My precious son (LUWB) for inspiring me to live a significant life,

Family (especially Auntie & Uncle) and friends, particularly my dearest sister-friends, whose support carried me through the most difficult times;

Spiritual parents, Dr. La Fayette and Theresa Scales for the life you talk and walk,

Visionaries, Dr. David and the late Pastor Darlene Kandole, who glimpsed my destiny and spoke it forth.

Bishop Ward, the wind beneath my wings for this project and Sis. Becky for understanding how we are,

Tiny Communications, LLC, for cover and logo designs;

Dr. Valerie Lee and Denise Goldstein for editing services;

My cheering squad who encouraged me.

I love and appreciate all of you immensely.

Chapter One

In The Garden

Certainly, everyone enters their relational garden with the highest hopes and concerted effort to sustain flourishing relationships with friends, business partners, co-workers, neighbors and spouses. However, we do not choose the family we are born into; nor do we have the option to write-off family members as we sometimes may contemplate doing with others. Like it or not, family is for keeps. This is why it is so important to adopt a Grace perspective that incorporates forgiveness.

My earliest recollection of family conflict was at the age of seven between my parents. My mother, who had the more fiery personality of the two, was upset over a disagreement with my father. Dad became a born-again believer six months before my birth and had recently acknowledged his call to ministry. Shortly after, he started attending bible college, taking leadership roles in church groups and supporting services at churches affiliated with ours. Then one Sunday morning as Dad was rushing to get to church, Mom said, *"I'm sick and tired of you leaving me to get the kids ready while you run off to get your seat in the front row!"* Dad sternly responded, *"that's where I'm supposed to be; you should be happy you have a husband who goes to church."* Observing her vulnerability and the emotional debris of their 'intense moment of fellowship,' I lead her by the hand to a large pink chair in our living room, and said, *"Mommy, let's pray."*

Months later my mother also gave her life to Christ. Yet, their polar opposite personalities fueled the flame between them. Nevertheless, as they made adjustments in their marital roles and family responsibilities, I saw something in their marriage that clearly indicated they were committed to their relationship, family and faith. I learned what it meant to disagree intensely and remain tenaciously cemented through forgiveness, love and commitment to each other. What I did not understand as much was why two people in love, passionately disagreed in the first place. My Alice-in-Wonderland worldview did not leave space for arguments among friends and family. Today's TV melodramas in which families fight over everything from sexual orientation to sushi provide poor models of family unity.

Yet, clearly, the family environment is the incubator for future relationships and provides the template for how we deal with conflict. While my oldest brother did not seem as keenly aware of the hidden dynamics of our parents' relationship, I came wired with a predisposition for curious inquiry into why people act like they do. Naturally, my most ardent investigative endeavors involved the individuals I called Mom and Dad. I quietly observed, questioned and contemplated the weightier matters of relational dynamics. For example, while playing, I would engage in social role-play over issues affecting my parents with varied outcomes.

On one occasion, I was role-playing a scene in my bedroom involving a visit to the OB/GYN while in the third trimester; as was my mother carrying my youngest brother. To get into character, I meticulously rolled up a pliable pillow and tucked it into my shirt, making sure to perfectly replicate the distended curvature of Mom's pregnant belly. As I was leaving home (my room), to go to the doctor's office (my parents' room), my mother came upstairs and caught me en route. She did not get the drama or the role I was playing. She scolded me based on her interpretation of my intent. I was angry for both being misunderstood and her inability to appreciate my imaginative, Oscar-worthy costume. Most conflicts start in similar fashion over a misunderstanding or misinterpretation of someone else's actions or intent.

I responded by withdrawing and being sullen for a few days. This pattern, which continued for many years, laid a formidable foundation for what came next when I encountered conflict. While the enemy was trying to erect emotional barricades, God was fashioning the weapons of warfare in my hands against relational enemies such as; strife, division, bitterness, resentment and unforgiveness.

By the time I was in fifth grade, I had a basketful of experiences dealing with peer conflict. My pudgy little body had sprouted into a tall, rather gangly physique, which drew taunts and teasing from other children. After weeks of being called "beanpole", "string bean" and "tree", I returned home from the war zone emotionally battered and bruised. Mom readily discerned my fallen spirit as I retreated to my room one day. She called me downstairs to the living room to ask details about my social encounters at school. Upon giving her my explanation, she told me I had to *learn* how to deal with other children and situations. She started first with the internal state of my mind containing thoughts and appraisals of me, which were predominantly negative.

I remember vividly her reaching for a magazine with a black actress' face on the front cover, dramatically pointing at it and telling me I could be anything I wanted to be if I did not let other people define me. She also emphasized the need to see myself as she and Dad saw me — their beautiful, chocolate-dipped little girl who they loved very much. Further, she admonished me to look into the mirror of God's eyes where I could see who I really was and would become. Then, she said, *"You won't fall prey to the appraisals of others."* At that moment, I did not fully register how powerful this affirmation was and its effect on my life.

In the immediate future, my confidence soared as I gained some skills in dealing with social pressure and criticism. Shortly after, I noticed the kids who regularly teased me started backing off. I believe my parents prayed and asked God to show me how to overcome fear, courageously deal with conflict and forgive. Sometimes, I still wanted to retreat. After all, I knew how to do that well. Yet, I could hear Mom's voice and see her finger striking that magazine cover in the face of a beautiful Black woman who had overcome many obstacles. Likewise, I observed Mom in various social situations, her transformation in Christ, and in like manner, I wanted to be an overcoming woman.

WISDOM LESSONS LEARNED

Love and commitment go hand in hand, you cannot really love without being committed.

We are defined by an accurate perception of self which comes from God, not the perception of others.

What parents say and do has a lasting impact on their child.

WISEWORD - Proverbs 22:6

Train up a child in the way he should go; and when he is old, he will not depart from it.

Chapter Two

I Just Don't Like You

As the first couple on Eden Avenue, minding their own business, came into contact with a foe that did not like them, so I met many two-legged reptiles who liked me even less.

It is usually not anything we do that brings disdain from someone else. It could be as crazy as they do not like the way you walk, smile or part your hair. People have all kinds of issues brewing inside their hearts, which play out in the mind and shape their perceptions in social encounters with other people. Such was the case in junior high school.

After finishing elementary school at a private Christian school, my oldest brother and I were bused to a predominately White junior high school everyday with other Black children from diverse cultural backgrounds. Up to this point, my life had been sterile. I went from home to school, back home, to church, school and church again. Mom and Dad provided a beautifully furnished home in which my brothers and I took harbor. Literally, Mom's protectiveness extended to her installing a perimeter gate around our house and a basketball court for my brothers to play on. Her logic was the neighborhood kids could come to our house to play, thereby enabling her to keep a close eye on our friends and us.

In retrospect, this was not all bad. We had many friends in our quiet middle-class neighborhood, but gates cannot keep snakes out. They are everywhere people gather and my junior high was open territory with another level of challenge.

I got a job working in the cafeteria serving on the food line. As peers came through, they sometimes asked me for extra goodies because I sat with them during my free period or in study hall. I tried to explain I would not keep my job if I was caught giving away free food. Nevertheless, this did not go over well with some of them. I recall one group of older girls threatened if I did not sneak them extra sandwiches when they came through the line the next day, they were going to do something to me. It just so happened I also had gym class with these girls. I was horrified, but did not tell my brother or parents.

The next day came with lightening speed and they stood in front of me awaiting their extra sandwiches. My skinny legs were shaking so hard, I could almost feel the bones moving underneath my skin. I handed each one a sandwich, while trying to ignore their dagger-like glares. I felt the sweat on my neck drip down between my shoulder blades as I imagined their response.

The two periods between lunch and gym provided little relief from the sickening fear knotted in my stomach. I walked to the gymnasium in slow motion, hearing their threats blaring in my head like the morning announcements over the PA system.

I entered the gym, headed directly to the lockers to put my stuff up and change into gym clothes. I bent down to tie my shoestrings; then looked up to find myself surrounded by vipers.

One girl, who I barely knew, started asking me questions, *"Who do you think you are, don't you know we can beat the sh_t out of you?"*

They all looked like they could and would if I did not think of something fast. However, I could barely breathe, let alone think. I only knew how petrified I was.

Then, my cactus dry lips parted to form a question out of nowhere, *"Why are you guys doing this?"*

I was stunned when another girl answered for all of them, *"Cause, I just don't like you."*

While trying to think of a response, the second bell rang and our teacher yelled, *"Everybody to the gym now!"*

I was literally saved by the bell from God only knows what. Still, this did not mean the problem was solved. I had to, as my mother warned, learn how to deal with the situation. By this time, I had been a Christian for several years and knew how to pray. So, my prayer was very practical — God, keep those girls from hurting me. I was not too concerned about learning any lessons in conflict resolution or about forgiveness. I just wanted to get home safe. God answered my prayer — I got home safe. However, when I opened my book bag, I found my shattered glasses. I did not want to tell my parents because I knew they would intervene by informing the Principal, who in turn would do an investigation. Once those girls got in trouble, it would be more trouble for me.

From that moment on, I realized something very profound about the human condition; we all have the potential for evil in our heart if it is not yielded to God's Word. Those girls did not even know me really, yet they determined in their hearts not to like me. Conflict develops in the heart and mind; it is not outside but inside of us. I had a choice to make: I could either retaliate (if only in my mind), retreat in an attempt to avoid the problem, or find a way to turn the tide.

If I did not know anything else about our home, I knew it was a house of prayer. My parents hosted prayer band meetings frequently and family prayer was regular. So I did what seemed natural — I asked God to show me what to do to change this situation so I would not have to go to school everyday fearful of getting the stuffing taken out of my backside.

I remember praying so hard one night, I actually believed I heard God answer me audibly, *"Call a meeting with the girls and have your gym teacher, who almost everybody likes, sit in."* I went to my teacher first and told her what happened. She was sympathetic yet clueless as to how she could help beyond keeping an eye out for potential trouble in class. As I began to unfold her role in helping me, she affirmed my mature response and committed to convene a meeting after our next gym class in a couple of days.

While awaiting the meeting, I imagined something good would come out of it and maybe I could even be a friend to these girls. Perhaps it was Pollyanna-ish to think one alternate encounter could change their hearts concerning me, but I was optimistic.

My teacher convened the meeting as she promised and the girls sat silently as she unfolded details of the incident in the gym and my broken glasses. She invited me to tell them how I felt about what happened. I told them I liked them, was not mad about what they did and wanted to be friends. To my surprise and hers, they listened. I even saw a glimmer of remorse in one girl's teary eyes. Our teacher, observing this also, told us how she wanted her students to be a unified community wherein we all learned to appreciate the uniqueness of each other. We sat for a moment in silence after she spoke, then spontaneously I reached out my hand to the girl who said she didn't like me. She hung her head and responded by grasping my hand and we both started crying. Our teacher asked each of us to hug and she hugged us while telling us we were good girls. The bell rang and we left together to catch the bus home.

For the rest of junior high, I never had any trouble with those girls. Yes, there were times I recalled the hurt inflicted by their bullying and had to forgive them all over again. Herein lies the major point of the lesson God was teaching me. Forgiveness is not a one-time deal. Instead, it is like the ebb and flow of ocean tides, each wave erodes the stones of bitterness and resentment and opens the way for deeper levels of forgiveness, intimacy and renewal.

My next significant encounter was with a 'king cobra'. One day as I reported to the cafeteria for work, a boy greeted me in the dimly lit hallway just inside the door. When I walked in, I felt a foreboding uneasiness.

As I proceeded to hang up my sweater and put on a smock, he stepped close behind me and whispered in my ear, *"Can I finger you?"*

Penned between the coat rack and his body, I could only move just enough to turn around. In a split second, I came face-to-face with another evil I had never encountered. I tried to buy time to think by asking him what he meant, and his reply was equally disarming — *"Let me show you."*

There was no negotiation or mediation except by the Holy Spirit. Instantly, I was rescued from this situation when I slapped him so hard the black fell off his face. As he reached up to grab his smarting cheek, I shoved him out of my way and ran to my workstation. I told the lady who worked alongside me what happened and she reported it to her boss, who in turn told the Principal. After he heard my story, that boy was suspended for several days. When he returned to school, he never bothered me again.

WISDOM LESSONS LEARNED

You can like people even when they do not like you.

What is in my heart can influence a change in someone else's.

People can change for the better in the midst of conflict.

Some conflicts come to an instant resolve with one strategic action.

WISEWORD - Matthew 5: 44

But I say unto you, Love your enemies, bless them that curse you, do good to them that hate you, and pray for them which despitefully use you, and persecute you.

Chapter Three

Let It Shine

The transition from junior to senior high was relatively smooth. I was a solid student, with good study habits, so the extra load of the college prep curriculum was not too difficult. Conversely, my social skills were still developing so I was not the most popular kid on the block. Nevertheless, for some odd reason, another girl who was quite popular befriended me. Our Oscar-Felix friendship worked well because we accepted and appreciated each other's unique personality. By this time, God was also tugging at my heart relative to being an example among my peers, many of whom were using drugs, alcohol and were sexually active.

Even with temptations to follow suit with them, my sights were on college and beyond. Furthermore, I was scared of disappointing my parents, most especially Dad who, by now, I had developed a closer relationship. Mom played a major role in shaping my femininity and vision for a professional career in the field of my choice, while Dad focused on my spiritual development. I asked for his advice on everything from boys to boots. He never judged or criticized my thinking even when it was totally off. It was as though we were simultaneously growing up in Lord, me on my level and he on his. I watched closely as he handled conflict while multi-tasking in his role as husband, father, employee, entrepreneur and minister, with an unwavering commitment to boldly living the Gospel.

One afternoon as I sat in my favorite class, a girl I did not know well started asking questions about why I did not hang out with my girlfriend's wild friends. I was shocked because I did not think anyone was paying much attention to notice any difference between me and other kids at school. After all, I was not wearing a cross around my neck, carrying a Bible in my book bag or even talking about God, so I pondered for a nanosecond why she asked the question.

Truth is, I was a closet Christian that was not trying to come out anytime soon. Do not get me wrong, I thoroughly enjoyed going to church, singing in the choir, ushering and holding leadership positions in my youth group. I just did not think it necessary to close the breach between Church and State. In reality, I was trying to avoid conflict because I did not want to be ridiculed, or have to debate or defend my beliefs—especially if it meant more taunts and teasing.

I may have healed some from the former bruises, yet I still had the scars. My aim was a serene high school existence.

Still, I gave her an honest answer, which she put on blast and it spread around the school like wildfire. I wanted to retreat, but all the closet doors were nailed shut. It was a well-known fact and could not be converted to fiction. She told people I was a "goodie-goodie girl" and next thing I knew, I was being talked about. High school then was not like it is now, where kids are into so many offbeat things no one really cares what someone is trying to be. However, then every little difference was noted and if it was weird, you were labeled as such. Being a Christian was a standout thing other kids did not understand or appreciate.

Then another encounter occurred while sitting in study hall. A group of girls made statements about how boring and strict my life must be. In an effort to avoid more criticism, I began to tell them about all the activities I was involved in at church, hoping to convince them I did 'cool' things too. They did not readily buy this because they were already aware of churchgoers' prohibitions against things they enjoyed doing. I felt isolated and alone. Then something unusual happened a few days later. One of the girls asked me about my youth group. Sensing her interest, I enthusiastically told her about an upcoming event and casually invited her.

To my surprise, she came, enjoyed herself and from then on, we talked often. She grew increasingly

17

more curious and open to me sharing my faith. We continued to spend our study hall period talking with other friends who, because of her influence, became less hostile toward this Christian. Over time, there were many occasions to demonstrate God's love as they faced challenges in their families and peer relationships. I became a sounding board for everything from courses to boys, most especially with my popular girlfriend, who was head-over-heels with boys. I discovered an enjoyment for helping people with problems by giving the wise counsel my parents had imparted into me to them.

Thanks to one girl's bold question, life was anything but serene; especially senior year when this unpopular kid was voted to represent my class as a part of the Senior Cabinet. The light in my heart was on high beam as I did like that little song sung in Sunday school:

"This little light of mine, I'm gonna let it shine,

this little light of mine, I'm gonna let it shine,

this little light of mine, I'm gonna let it shine;

let it shine, let it shine, let it shine."

WISDOM LESSONS LEARNED

The high cost of conflict avoidance is loss of opportunities to share what is important to you.

Someone is always observing you even when you do not think so.

The place of greatest influence is with those you least expect.

God's plan for our life supersedes our personality, faults and self-perception.

WISEWORD - Matthew 5:16 (TNIV)

In the same way, let your light shine before others, that they may see your good deeds and glorify your Father in heaven.

Chapter Four

Can We All Just Get Along!

S ummer flew by and next thing I knew I was on campus exploring new sights, sounds and people. Recalling the transition, there were some difficult places as my parents' emotional reaction to the impending departure was quite different. Mom tried to convince me to stay home and enroll in a local college within walking distance, while Dad was confident wherever I went, God would meet me there. He tried to help Mom accept that another one of their little chicks had developed its wings and was ready to take flight; but she still took it hard.

I saw the Heavenly father's tenderness working through Dad as he prepared all of us for the coming shifts. While my excitement over going to college nearly swept me away, I was also sensitive to Mom's feelings. I wanted her to be happy and excited, not sad. Therefore,

I prayed and kept preparing. A few days before our short road trip, Dad called me to his office to give affirmations and admonishments. I still remember to this day what he told me: *"I have every confidence in the Holy Spirit to keep you, if you want to be kept. Ask God for wisdom, obey and trust Him and you won't go wrong. Keep yourself pure — remember, we are sending you to college to get a B.A. not a B A B Y."* He stood, anointed my head with oil, prayed over me, hugged and kissed me.

Freshman year, I fully committed to my new-found freedom. Staying up late hanging out with new friends or making 3 A.M. pizza runs was par for the course. No one to monitor my coming and going was outrageously exhilarating. I almost emptied my bladder when I thought about it. I was determined to get an advanced degree even before graduating high school, so naturally good grades were paramount. Yet, I also thought it was important to enjoy college life.

The biggest shift was sharing a living space with another creature I did not know. I had my own room back home and never considered sharing with someone else. My roommate was a pretty, vibrant and highly social young woman, of Italian heritage. She had grown up in a small Pennsylvanian town with limited contact with Black people. On the other hand, because of my exposure to people of diverse ethnic and cultural backgrounds while traveling cross-country with Dad to speaking engagements, I was comfortable rooming with someone of a different ethnicity. She was curious about everything, most especially my hair. My ability to manipulate my kinky locks into so many style variations simply amazed her. I explained,

Black woman are versatile in many ways and encouraged her to get to know the other sisters on campus so she would not rely solely on me for her Black History course. She did not follow this suggestion, so I had to patiently endure her constant barrage of questions, comments and sometimes even criticisms. Additionally, her social life began to erode the boundaries of our living space.

For example, since home was only 45 minutes away, I frequently left campus for weekends. I returned to campus early one Sunday afternoon, entered my room and found one of my roomie's friends and her boyfriend lying in my bed. My neck got so hot you could have fried Canadian bacon on it. Even worse, at the moment I entered the room, my roommate was not there, so it read to me as not only a violation of my personal space, but of my sense of security because I was not sure if my roommate gave them a key. Of course, the startled couple got right up and left, yet the damage was already done.

By the time my roommate showed up, I was angry and had regressed to an earlier coping mechanism of emotional withdrawal. She was either very perceptive or had already been tipped off by her friend. When she asked me what was wrong, I could hardly form the words to express how violated I felt. As it goes, most conflicts result from a perceived or real threat to physical, emotional or even spiritual safety. It is sometimes hard for someone who also fears rejection, ridicule or abandonment to venture down a familiar road of confrontation. Such was my case. College life is as much about social assessment as academic assessment. On a small campus such as mine, a reputation can be difficult to live down, so I was afraid to say the wrong thing.

My roommate was already socially well connected and offending her could affect relationships across sectors of my social niche. Yet, previous experiences had taught me valuable lessons about the positive outcome of conflict versus the damaging results of smoldering, unresolved conflict. Therefore, I pried my lips apart to say *"I am very upset."* From there, a wellspring of words gushed forth until I could not say anything else. I was more hurt over being disrespected than I was angry. Fortunately, she seemed to get that and without attempting to minimize my feelings, she apologized.

Wow! I was shocked; she was really invested in our relationship and her response showed it. From here, we established a clear understanding relative to how we would handle entertaining friends in our room, especially when one of us was absent. We agreed our respect for each other's personal living space would not be compromised to accommodate visitors. Our lengthy talk was sealed with a tearful embrace. I learned something that evening about our relationship and myself I had not realized until then: relationships are more important than my being comfortable. Meaning, I would rather fight *for* a relationship than lose one for fear of fighting. My home away from home was peaceful from then on and laid a foundation for what came next.

During sophomore year, a community conflict erupted between Black and White students over racially charged comments. At that time, the total Black population was less than 50 of approximately 2000 students. While the President's office, Dean of Students and Faculty tried to champion diversity on campus, minorities were conspicuously missing among students, staff and faculty. The white-bean soup environment now lightly sprinkled with pepper, was not necessarily seasoned to everyone's taste. As tensions mounted, so did misunderstandings, misinterpretations and blatant offenses.

Things got so bad, Black students stopped hanging out with their White friends. The Black Student Union (BSU) became more vocal in its complaints to Administration and initiated a protest in front of the administration building. I remember being horrified one morning when a loud pounding on my door awakened my roommate and me. I opened the door to the face of two Black males insisting I hurriedly dress and come to the BSU lounge for an emergency strategy meeting. All of a sudden, I saw a news headline flash in front of my eyes: *Local preacher's daughter arrested in riotous takeover of a campus building.* My parents would have a cow!

My frightened roommate pleaded with me not to go. I was scared out of my skin; yet, went anyway. The meeting was blistering with heated emotions, and again, I thought about retreating home for a few days in hopes all would calm down. But it would take more than a few days to reverse the boisterous storms hitting my campus.

When communities collide, it is difficult for everyone, most especially someone who had attachments in both camps as I did. Raised a people-lover, I was taught to be loyal in friendship, to honor, respect and appreciate the uniqueness of everyone's ethnic and cultural background. My parents modeled it, so I knew it was possible.

I was pressed into my first campus leadership role when the President handpicked a group of students to be trained as small group facilitators to guide other students in meaningful dialogue over diversity issues. Recalling Dad's admonishment, *"If you see a problem, then be a part of the solution,"* I readily accepted. I completed the training while trying to understand what exactly God was doing. Within a few days, something horrible jumped off — a black colored figure was found hanging from a tree with a noose around its neck. My God, it was like my campus had been torpedoed leaving emotional shrapnel strewn about everywhere.

Ready or not, the student facilitators were deployed when the President called for several campus-wide open discussions. In one of these forums, student and faculty emotions were flying like air missiles. It was as if overhead bombs would take us all out, when suddenly I stood up and shouted, *"CAN WE ALL JUST GET ALONG!"*

The jarring statement produced deafening silence for a brief moment as everyone contemplated the simplistic act of our wills to peacefully co-habit our microcosmic world. Unfortunately, it was not that simple. It would take the transformation of hearts, minds and wisdom to accomplish this. None of which could happen without divine intervention. Well acquainted with accessing the divine, I began to pray for my campus and mobilized a few like-minded students to do the same as a covert strategy to reclaim territory seized by hatred and strife.

As you can imagine, change was a slow process. However, the atmosphere shifted as prayer-pressure was applied to fortresses of bitterness, resentment, malice and unforgiveness. Looking back now, this is where I cut my wisdom teeth in taking spiritual authority over dominions in these areas. Inch by inch, progress was made as people put down their instruments of war to reach for peace. I assumed other leadership positions that gave me access to greater levels of influence with peers, administrators and faculty to whom I spoke openly about the transformative power of God's love and its operation in healing racial wounds.

Then, much to my surprise, I was asked by a committee comprised of faculty and administrators if I thought my uncle, a community activist back home, would consider a position on the university's Board of Trustees. I said he might if asked. When asked, he accepted, and became the first Black person to join (and subsequently became a lifetime Board member). He nearly single-handedly changed the hue of the racial fabric by heavily recruiting large numbers of talented Black students.

I graduated with a double major BA in one hand and a higher degree of spiritual aptitude in the other. No longer afraid, this young warrior was released into the world.

Life is so poetically rhythmical; the very week this chapter was written, my dear Uncle passed away. Therefore, it is dedicated to his memory.

WISDOM LESSONS LEARNED

The worth of any relationship is determined by a willingness to fight for it.

Great leaders stand up when all else has fallen down.

One pebble thrown into the pond makes great waves.

Change is good and transformation is even better.

WISEWORD- 1 Corinthians 15:58 (TNIV)

Therefore, my dear brothers and sisters, stand firm. Let nothing move you. Always give yourselves fully to the work of the Lord, because you know that your labor in the Lord is not in vain.

Chapter Five

More Than A Notion

Three months after graduation, I landed a professional position as a Social Worker for a county children's services agency. I started in the Crisis Unit and loved working with families.

My naïve save-the-world perspective changed quickly as I encountered situations which stretched me emotionally and spiritually. Even though I punched in at nine and out by five, I took the job home.

I worried about my clients and their ability to practically apply counsel given relative to their crisis. I soon realized most of what I did was patchwork until the next explosive event, because habitual relational patterns were not going to change just because an energetic, young social worker intervened. Like the change I observed on my campus, change in their lives would be a slow process, requiring successive reinforcement from many sources.

In addition to my job experiences, I continued to explore the freedom of young adulthood by expanding my community involvement and socializing with other professionals, inclusive of dating. Up to now, I had not dated and was naïve about the open market of the local singles scene. I lived with my parents, so for the most part anyone I associated with regularly was still scrutinized by them. However, upon acquiring my first vehicle, they had less opportunity to observe all of the spaces and places of my exploration in this area.

I also had not noticed how attractive I had become. From Mom, I inherited a natural tendency toward tasteful fashion and adorned myself to my liking — not necessarily to catch a man's eye. As a sidebar for my female reader, I think we should dress for ourselves not men and model what godly femininity really is for the younger generation of girls. Perhaps then we can change the tide of the scantily clad butts and boobs on display everywhere; but then of course, we have to tuck in our stuff too. Yes, I said it.

My job was located downtown within walking distance of large department stores, which for this 'fashionista' was dangerous. While visiting one store on lunch break, I stopped in the Men's Furnishing Department to quickly spot a nice gift for Dad before shooting off to ladies suits and dresses. An Adonis-look-alike approached me and asked if I needed assistance. I really did not as I was only browsing and, unbeknownst to me, he was too.

A brief conversation and he had my name and where I worked — naïve and more dangerous than a credit card. A few days later, the secretary patched a call through from him. He asked if he could call me after work and I agreed. After several phone conversations and passing initial screening, I accepted a lunch invitation. We met at a quaint downtown café a few doors from my job. He picked me up at the office, which had my female co-workers buzzing. During lunch, I lightly queried him again on his goals and relationship with God.

The following week, he asked me to dinner at a casual restaurant similar to Applebee's. Since I was not ready to introduce him to my parents, I suggested we meet there. Halfway through dinner, I discerned something in the Spirit; but could not label it. Of course, then, I would not have called it discernment because I was not as aware of the spiritual gifts and manifestations as I am now. All I knew was something was not right about this guy. By God's design, my work turned hectic and left me drained. It was all I could do to drive home, eat, go to bed only to wake up the next day and do it all over again. We talked more by phone, which put enough distance between the forest and me to see the trees.

I was heavily involved in my church, attended small group Bible studies and excited about my salvation. I shared this exuberance with people I met and invariably included an invitation to my church. After several unsuccessful attempts to interest him in coming, I really wondered what is up with a guy who says he loves God, but irregularly attends his own church, has never invited me to his and will not come to mine. I was frustrated and confronted him about it. His resistance met my persistence and sparks flew. One evening, he flat out told me off for inquiring once again about his spirituality. According to him, he was a "good person" because he did not drink alcohol, smoke, or go to clubs and that was enough to make him hell-proof (my words, not his).

Then one day at work, the secretary told me she saw him at a club over the weekend 'nasty dancing' with a woman. That did it for me. It was then I realized the feeling I had on our second date was more than a notion. It was Holy Spirit discernment. I let him call persistently for several days without response until the elixir of infatuation wore off. When I told him what I heard, he said it was no big deal and asked me to come to the club with him. I told him I would come to the club, when he comes to my church. Years later I saw him and he was still the same person, doing the same thing.

WISDOM LESSONS LEARNED

Thankfully, God does not always give us what we think we want.

Before going shopping make a list and stick to it.

When meeting someone ask the Holy Spirit three questions before advancing forward:

    1) Who Is This Person?
    2) Who Sent Him or Her?
    3) For What Purpose?

WISEWORD - Proverbs 3:6

In all thy ways acknowledge him, and he shall direct thy paths.

Chapter Six

Ribbon in the Sky

I did not date for the next few years and watched girlfriends get married one by one. In fact, some of my friends who married early had thriving marriages. One day while visiting one of these couples, the husband — an aspiring attorney, who happened to be my accountant — suggested I attend a get-together with some young professionals. Most of the people there would be his law school peers. He told me upfront his plan to introduce me to a friend and predicted we would hit it off. His wife, who had been my college English professor, giggled, and like Sarah, I laughed at the prospect.

We clicked immediately, finishing each other's sentences and catching the wind between our thoughts. I could hardly believe I met someone who seemed to get me. Over several weeks, our lengthy conversations fired up phones lines as a melodious fusion of mind and heart played like a well-rehearsed orchestra. Love bug bit and neither of us looked for a remedy. It was Eden, its entire splendor with no reptiles in sight.

My parents soon caught wind of the young man constantly calling for me, so a formal introduction was in order. I will never forget how terrified I was when my new friend showed up at my door for his first meeting with Dad. By then, I was already quite smitten and did not want him to get the axe. I introduced them and they disappeared to the den behind closed doors. On the other side, I seemed to sweat drops of blood during the hour-long caucus. When they emerged, my friend looked well worked over. Dad passed some pleasant comments and showed him to the front door. Then he nudged me into the den for a fireside chat as he frequently did throughout my teen years. He gave me instructions, encouragement, admonishment or corrections depending on the situation. On this occasion, he reiterated his vision for our family and me specifically, then advised me to travel slowly — never driving ahead of my spiritual headlights. He asked how I felt about my friend, as if the blush on my face had not already answered the question. We were allowed to court (Dad did not like the word "date") under parental supervision.

Fast forward a year and a half. I heard mention of marriage. My heart leaped at the possible realization of the dream — marrying my tall, dark and handsome prince in a large church wedding, two children and love ever after. In my mind, the plan was all laid out.

However, I did not fully consider what God wanted or what He was doing. Surely, He would co-sign my pursuit of the proverbial good life. Was it not His desire after all, for two people to consummate their love in marriage?

We are both Christians, intelligent and ambitious, which should be enough fuel to move this ship forward, I thought. He asked Dad for my hand, then turned to me for my answer to *"Will you marry me?'* The moment was surreal; this is really happening every cell inside shouted. *Yes, Yes, Yes!* I jumped to my feet, reached for the phone to call important people in my life. His pearly whites lit up the room like xenon headlights on a pitch-black night.

Within weeks, major wedding plans like date, time and location were made. Mom moved with locomotive speed, scouting out New York boutiques for the perfect dress. She arrived back from the first trip with pictures, fabric swatches and prices. The groom-to-be, hidden beneath a lofty spray of law books, tucked his head out every now and again to give his opinion on the plans.

Six months zoomed by, things started to get serious. We felt the pressure of the soon approaching date, tensions mounted and emotions heated. We had our first of many arguments, but everyone said it was pre-wedding jitters. Jitters or not, I did not like arguing. I thought love was not supposed to yell, get angry or look mean. Who wants to fight with the person who will soon share your bed?

My parents were married over thirty years by then, and even in their moments of passionate discussion, I saw love. Mom's lioness personality was tamed by Dad's teddy bear, serene temperament. It was always about family solidarity and marital accord. It meant someone taking the royal road by stepping down and not asserting his or her rights. It meant submission and obedience not only from Mom, but from Dad too, who often said, *"The way up is down."* I had a model and wanted my marital house to be built of the same brick and mortar.

After an outstanding wedding day under a cerulean sky with a golden ribbon in it, we headed off into the sunset happily married. Our early days were filled with adjustments to life together blending aspects of our temperament and personalities. My husband was more outgoing than me; so, we frequently entertained guests in our tastefully decorated home.

As time passed, after the guests left and the last candle was blown out, our relationship started to look less like the bright mosaic I had in mind and I saw my husband's vision blurred by the realities of marriage also. Our trajectories were diverging not converging. Still, we were firmly connected to family and a host of friends who viewed us like the Black Princess Diana and Prince Charles. We welcomed all the public attention, but found less solace outside of their admiring gaze. The cross-stitch thread of hope was that each day would bring us closer to our dreams, and in some ways, it did;

however, there were many nightmares woven between and the ribbon in the sky was rapidly fraying.

Five years post-ceremony, we were like two boxers in their respective corners of the ring, our gloves were adjusted, the bell blasted and we came out slugging. Oh, there is no one person to blame, only our unsurrendered souls filled with selfish ambition, unmet needs and unresolved issues hidden beneath the polished veneer of intellect and ambitious endeavor.

Our baby's advent seemed to reunite us in anticipation and nursery preparation, while friends and family looked on with great excitement. Our little bundle of joy was born without medical event on a beautiful, sunlit Sunday afternoon. The splendor of God's love and grace was present as he traversed the birth canal. I had prayed and believed for a boy — my faith was rewarded.

Parenthood did little to alleviate the animosity between us as we argued about everything from caregivers for the baby to who he favored most. I finally realized, we fought more than we fellowshipped, or at least it appeared that way. After a while, both of us were dangling on the ropes dazed by emotional blows. With the added pressures of new motherhood, I was rapidly coming unglued.

Life is humorous. I was in graduate school working toward a doctorate in psychology while so depressed, I needed counseling and meds myself. With God's help, I withstood my emotions to stay focused on taking care of our baby and completing my studies.

41

Instead of medication, I called Daddy probably eight times daily just to maintain some sanity. He consoled, corrected and challenged me to focus my eyes on Jesus through prayer, take care of myself, the baby and let God handle my problems. It was hard. Problems I could see. Jesus, I could not. Yet, his sound counsel always steered me in the right direction, so I made my best effort to follow the road map.

Soon, I realized I needed a dose increase because I could not function on ten minutes a day spent with the Lord. I began to see that the marital problems were partially because I was not praying much and even less for my husband. Truthfully, I liked him less than I prayed for him; and justified my reasons for these feelings.

Before long however, supernatural events grabbed my attention and brought me to my knees. The details of the gory marital stuff is not worth recounting, but suffice it to say, there was stinky garbage in the garden. Intellect had failed to pull me through and I needed a touch from God — his instruction and wisdom. I had never really prayed for wisdom; only the resolution of whatever problem I faced. My prayers consisted of asking for a prescription to alleviate the symptoms instead of a cure for the underlying cause. Then, I started hearing messages about the wisdom of God and asking for it without doubt or unbelief.

WISDOM LESSONS LEARNED

If you are lost, get a road map and follow it.

Don't drive ahead of your spiritual headlights.

WISEWORD - James 1:5 (TNIV)

If any of you lacks wisdom, you should ask God, who gives generously to all without finding fault, and it will be given to you.

Chapter Seven

Purpose from the Pain

After my husband and I separated, the pain was so intense I needed a heavy-duty spiritual painkiller to make it through each day. I started reading my Bible, fasting and praying regularly, and my flesh revolted. My soul, which had been on self-propel up to this point, did not like it too much either. I did not know then what I know now about the soul's content and its effect on our behavior. Paradoxically, I had not connected my fascination with psychology, which examines the soul, to the spiritual journey I was on. God's orchestration of our lives is incredible. He does not waste any opportunity to teach His children truths about themselves and Him. I was getting an advanced spiritual degree in many ways.

During this time, I dreamed prolifically in detail and living color. I remember a dream wherein I stood in my kitchen, looking around, saw the kitchen counters all sparkling, the cabinets shining as though sunrays were beaming on them and everything was beautiful at eye level. Then I looked down at my feet where there was the most putrefied mess covering them. I could barely move for the mess. I was horrified at the sight!

Because God had dealt with me in dreams before, I knew enough to ask Him for an interpretation and to expect it. Within days, I understood the dream's meaning. The eye level beauty was everything people saw of me from the outside. While the mess around my feet represented what was in my heart and soul. Soul and heart issues were keeping me from moving forward. I would stay stuck where I was if I did not come face-to-face with a living God to take me from life on the surface, to a deeply profound understanding of Him, His ways, purpose for my life and my call to serve others. The latter would not be realized without the former being addressed.

I needed a relationship with the Godhead that was not relegated to a kid in a candy store with a parent, asking for goodies or having a tantrum because the request was not granted. Simply put, I needed to grow up. My marriage and subsequent divorce process were the conduit for this growth as God started speaking to me frequently about my stinkin' thinking, poor attitude and worse still, my immature behavior. I could not blame my husband for my plight because much of my soul's debris was well placed before he came on the scene. This production was already playing on the big screen and now God was rewriting the script. It was time to be transformed! Yes, my husband had his own bowl of issues, but that was beside the point. I had to examine myself and conflict was the rod on my back to get me to submit.

Even when I was not so cooperative, God allowed challenges to come my way to get my attention back on Him and soul cleansing. Usually these involved conflicts at work, with business constituents, or my developing son. A good example of this took place while I was serving as an interim department director for a local social services agency. When I stepped into the job, I assumed responsibility for supervising two employees and eight contractual professionals servicing the agency's clients. My staff was frustrated over poor communication with collaborators, which impeded the provision of services provided by my department. In all, the department was in disarray demonstrated by a faulty service delivery filing system, untimely payment of contractors and noncompliance with quarterly reporting. My primary focus was building a team and equipping my staff through instruction, constructive evaluation of job performance and praise to motivate them to serve in excellence. Within no time, we pulled our department together. Instead of this bringing congrats from my up-line supervisor, it brought disdain and our once pleasant relationship turned hostile. Whether she was jealous or intimidated by my supervisory success, I cannot say. What I do know, is spiritual assaults came fast and furious. Work samples, which at earlier stages in our relationship were applauded as excellent, now were being thrown back in my face to be re-done and submitted again. It seemed nothing I did pleased her. Then one day, she called me to her office and started venting about senior management inclusive of our Executive Director. I discerned this was a tactic to assess my loyalty by getting me to say something against senior administrators. When I did not take the bait, my work was subjected to greater scrutiny with persistent incidents of persecution. With each event, I had to look into the mirror of God's Word to evaluate the ugliness in my heart. I am talking about foul manure in the crevices of my soul that required a spiritual HazMat team—you know the expertly trained and equipped individuals who respond to the threat and/or deployment of nuclear, chemical and biological weapons of mass destruction. This is exactly what negative emotions like hatred, malice, strife, unforgiveness, contentions, uncontrolled anger, resentment and bitterness are, WEAPONS OF MASS DESTRUCTION TO OUR SPIRITUAL LIFE.

God loves us too much to let us self-destruct, terrorize or destroy others with these weapons. He worked on me, and is still at work, to keep me diligent in my pursuit of holiness and purity inwardly. In this situation, the Holy Spirit's instructions was to develop an attitude of gratitude for the job instead of complaining about my supervisor. God began to transform my heart attitude to sweet submission as I yielded to her demands. However, my staff, which was closely watching me, expressed anger about how I was being treated and did not understand why I did not 'stand up' to this corporate bully. I told them what the Holy Spirit told me: *"Keep your mouth shut unless I say otherwise."* Truly, silence is a powerful offensive weapon. Like they say, "if you don't start no mess, there won't be no mess."

Within weeks, my supervisor's animosity reached an all-time high, and she could not restrain her irrational anger. She stormed into my office, yelled a command at me and stated she was sick of supervising me. I prayed and received instruction to write a memo to my Executive Director. She responded by calling a meeting with a Board member, my supervisor and me. Upon entering the room, I noticed a tape recorder on the table and my Executive Director informed me of their intent to tape the meeting. I did not object. However, when my supervisor arrived, she vehemently objected and stormed out of the conference room while shouting, *"I never want to supervise her again!"* That was on a Friday; and on Monday afternoon the next week, my supervisor left work sick.

A few days later news spread around the agency that she was seriously ill and would not be returning to work   and she never did. I completed my assigned term there and was given a going-away party as if I had been with the agency for 25 years. My staff witnessed the transformation in me as I rode the pestilent waves of co-worker conflict and gave glory to God for the example set before them relative to how to handle similar situations. From this position, God promoted me when I won a major contract with the State of Ohio, which launched my own business!

Just about the time God ushered in this transition, major change was emerging in the marriage. Our embattled relationship was leading to dissolution, not resolution. However, this was far from what I wanted. I began to bargain with God and my husband to keep the status quo. Neither of them took the deal. God wanted my submission and obedience, and each was something I did not want to give up easily. Submit was a dirty, six letter word some women around me abhorred. It was not politically correct to even think in such terms in an academic culture where freedom of thought and action was highly valued. Therefore, even finding *Christian* women my age who fully embraced the Biblical principle of submission to God, much less their husband, was difficult.

Yet, nothing less would do. Divorce was imminent, and I cried out for relief from the internal war waging between my soul and spirit. This battle was going to be a fight to the finish, and the Spirit had to win for my survival.

In the midst of this mess, I was called into ministry. I thought God's timing was way off. Here I was soon to be a single, young mother, handling the rigors of graduate school and an emotional wreck. Nevertheless, I launched into the deep, added ministerial courses to my existing load of studies and on November 17, 1991, one year after my son's birth, I was birthed into ministry in Dad's pulpit. It was a bittersweet historical moment wherein my estranged husband was noticeably absent; yet, family and friends surrounded me, including a young couple that Dr. La Fayette Scales assigned to me to get me through the ordeal. This was truly a blessing itself because I was not attending Dr. Scales' church and had only visited once. Yet, as I received counsel from them, I learned more about marriage while divorcing. God has an interesting sense of humor.

For two years, the legal conflict was elevated to an all out war as our divorce was litigated in court. My heart was infected with anger, resentment, malice and unforgiveness. Occasionally, I tried to convince myself I had forgiven him, but then something would happen and the destructive emotions would take over like a torrential flood. It was literally impossible for me to talk or think about him without being consumed by these feelings. I knew it was unhealthy and sinful, but I did not know how to fully cleanse myself until I came across a book series by Liberty Savard. One of three books in the series entitled *Breaking the Power of Unmet Needs, Unhealed Hurts, Unresolved Issues in Your Life* gave me a prescription that would lay an axe to the root of these soul diseases. I submitted to surgery by cooperating with the Holy Spirit.

I have been divorced nearly sixteen years, have not remarried, and raised a son who is well connected to his dad. Yet, we still had residue between us and it affected our child. Yes, the open warfare had long since ended, yet little foxes would creep into the vineyard now and again. I was unaware of the process my ex was undergoing; but of course, I should have known God would pull the rope tight from both ends. He will have to pen his own book concerning his transformation. However, when our son reached high school, there were challenges associated with raising a teenager. Some of which we had to acknowledge were the result of what he saw in his parents' relationship. Here we were active in church and could not even get along with each other. Now, we had to join forces to battle for our seed. It was as if God purposefully fused us together to bring healing to old wounds.

From my observations of my ex-husband, it looked like he was also being pressed into submission, which affected how I received him when we talked. Little by little, the bricks began to topple and walls fell. Here recently, we started praying together for each other and our son, which brought a deeper level of intimacy. I remember the couple I counseled with during the divorce telling me *the most intimate thing couples can do is pray together.* It is true. When you pray in the Spirit for someone, your prayers are uncensored by your human intellect. Therefore, you will pray the purest prayer that touches God's throne regarding the other person. It is also impossible to stay angry with someone for whom you pray. As I consistently prayed for my ex-husband, I started seeing miraculous changes in my heart concerning him. I no longer held him hostage by my memories of old offenses. When I let go, I let God transform my entire perspective.

An example of this occurred this past Thanksgiving and Christmas holiday following the death of my mother-in-law. I lost Dad thirteen years ago, and Mom within the last six years, so I was well acquainted with the hurt he and his family were feeling. As Thanksgiving was approaching, my family planned to go South to visit my older sister. However, the Holy Spirit told me to stay home. When I told my ex-husband, he readily invited me to Thanksgiving dinner with his family, which would share this holiday without their mother. I went, and for the first time in my son's entire life, he was with both his parents to celebrate the holiday. Additionally, God used me to bring comfort and consolation to his family, who were equally happy to have me fellowshipping with them.

Then before our son came home for Christmas break, he asked me if he could bring a foreign student from Thailand with him from campus. I was delighted to have a visitor for the holidays — little did I know, God would sit another unexpected visitor at my table.

A few days before Christmas, I heard the Holy Spirit tell me to invite my ex-husband to brunch for the holiday. I did and he accepted. It was a double miracle! We were a family on Christmas. God is truly a God of reconciliation and restoration. This is, after all, what God sent His son to do — to reconcile and restore us to Him. It is remarkable what God can accomplish in the lives of people who yield their hearts to the redemptive power of forgiveness given to us by Jesus through His death on the cross. This is what the Grace-Full Model of Conflict Resolution entails: dying to self with all of our soul and heart issues, so we can extend grace to form and maintain relationships that reflect God's heart. I hope you will join me on the journey.

WISDOM LESSONS LEARNED

People are precious not perfect.

The sum total of life is relationships.

It is better to write offenses in sand, and cast love and forgiveness in marble.

People rise to the level of our prayers for them.

Painful situations are the incubators of purpose if we capture the lessons.

WISEWORD - 1 Peter 5: 10

And the God of all grace, who called you to his eternal glory in Christ, after you have suffered a little while, will himself restore you and make you strong, firm and steadfast.

Pass the Peace: The Garden Restored

When attending services at my Aunt and Uncle's church, there is a segment where the congregants "Pass the Peace." This involves greeting someone with an extended hand while saying, *"May the peace of the Lord be with you,"* and the receiver replies, *"And also with you."*

When is the last time you experienced real peace? I mean the kind of quiet confidence all is well, based on an inner knowing that God's hand is operating in your everyday life situations and relationships.

Truthfully, if you are like most of us, our sense of inner well-being can be fleeting when we encounter conflicts in relationships, or crisis in finances or faith. If we put too much emphasis on self instead of others, we are sure to make critical errors in judgment, which will likely exacerbate the situation. God directs our steps through life's journey to maximize our potential to come into the knowledge of who He is through relationship with Him and other people. Therefore, when we experience frustration, pain, grief, conflict or even traumatic loss, He extends His loving hand to us at a time when we are most vulnerable. This vulnerability opens us up to knowing God as the giver of all peace. How does this happen? The answer is simple — through a process. If you must hang a label on this process, its best described as "surrendering your soul" involving the submission of our mind, will, and emotions to God's will and purposes to manifest in and through each of us.

I am the first to admit, this process is not initially perceived as beneficial, which is why we find it so difficult to submit. Yet, as the process continues, it becomes increasingly clear our submission is necessary if we are to acquire knowledge, understanding and wisdom to help us ascend to the next level. So, whether your dream is to own a business, get an advanced degree or raise spiritually healthy children in a hedonistic world, we must be processed for our *divine purpose.* God's purpose for our lives must demand our full attention, because He jealously watches over His investment. To advance His righteous will on the earth as it is in Heaven, He cannot allow us to squander the wealth deposited in our unique personage. Therefore, as precious stones must be fired to achieve their rare brilliance and ultimate value, so must we be put through the fiery tests and trials of life to burn off anything hiding the radiant beauty of God's perfect design.

Perhaps it is difficult for you to see yourself as God's 'perfect design' because your life experiences have been far from perfect. Maybe you grew up in a home where you were abused, neglected, or abandoned. You may have come to believe you are damaged goods and worthless. My friend, this is a LIE! Again, using the analogy of precious stones, like a diamond, its value is revealed by the process it goes through. It is fired, polished, and then expertly cut to reflect light at multifaceted angles. This process is what differentiates a costly gemstone and cubic zirconium. The untrained eye may not readily discern the discrete difference, but the gemologist easily distinguishes between them. You are such a rare creation of God; you cannot measure yourself by others. God is the master gemologist discerning between the real and counterfeit. Hence, your only concern is staying in the process so increasingly more of His glory is revealed in you.

As we walk in our destiny path, God places people in our pathway to accelerate the process. This is why we should expectantly view each encounter as an opportunity to pass the peace. It does not necessarily mean every encounter will be with a pleasant person. Yet, it will, with our cooperation, yield lasting results when we learn required wisdom lessons. Perhaps you have a co-worker or boss who 'works your last nerve,' and all you can think about is getting another job so you no longer have to deal with that individual. Yet, if you look closely in his or her eyes, you will see the vacant longing of the soul for the kind of peace only God can offer. You, my friend were sent to the Kingdom for such a time as this. People everywhere are looking for peace that supersedes the chaos and pain inflicted by just living life. This is the very peace we are supposed to possess not for ourselves, but for those within our sphere of influence. Therefore, your irksome person needs what you have abiding within to facilitate the type of changes to help this individual walk in his or her destiny.

As the process continues, your perspective will change as your mind is transformed to see beyond your myopic needs to those of others. It is called the move from "me" to "we." I would venture to say, the divorce rate in America would drastically drop if more of us grasped this concept. Truly, my brothers and sisters, we must stop worshiping the "I" idol, which invariably leads to fighting and wars. We were placed in this earth to advance God's purposes by serving others and by the looks of things, we have some catching up to do. Our selfish desires and aspirations have dictated our decisions and behaviors far too long. It is a new day, time to take the gloves off and clasp our hands in prayer for God's wisdom to *pass the peace to restore the garden.*

WISDOM LESSONS LEARNED

What we consider a fiery trial is God's process of cutting and polishing us as His precious stones to radiate the brilliance of His glory in the earth.

The person who 'works your last nerve' is on a divine assignment to help you grow.

WISEWORD - Romans 12: 18

If it be possible, as much as lieth in you, live peaceably with all men.

COMPILATION OF WISDOM LESSONS LEARNED

Love and commitment go hand in hand, you cannot really love without being committed.

We are defined by an accurate perception of self which comes from God, not the perception of others.

What parents say and do has a lasting impact on their child.

You can like people even when they do not like you.

What is in my heart can influence a change in someone else's.

People can change for the better in the midst of conflict.

Some conflicts come to an instant resolve with one strategic action.

The high cost of conflict avoidance is loss of opportunities to share what is important to you.

Someone is always observing you even when you do not think so.

The place of greatest influence is with those you least expect.

God's plan for our life supersedes our personality, faults and self-perception.

Great leaders stand up when all else has fallen down.

One pebble thrown into the pond makes great waves.

The worth of any relationship is determined by a willingness to fight for it.

Change is good and transformation is even better.

Thankfully, God does not always give us what we think we want.

Before going shopping make a list and stick to it.

When meeting someone, ask the Holy Spirit three questions before advancing forward:
        1) Who Is This Person?
        2) Who Sent Him or Her?
        3) For What Purpose?

If you are lost, get a road map and follow it.

Don't drive ahead of your spiritual headlights.

People are precious not perfect.

The sum total of life is relationships.

It is better to write offenses in sand, and cast love and forgiveness in marble.

People rise to the level of our prayers for them.

Painful situations are the incubators of purpose if we capture the lessons.

What we consider a fiery trial is God's process of cutting and polishing us as His precious stones to radiate the brilliance of His glory in the earth.

The person who 'works your last nerve' is on a divine assignment to help you grow.

The Journey Continues . . .

The following manual and subsequent training will transform you, your marriage, family, workplace, church~ and community.

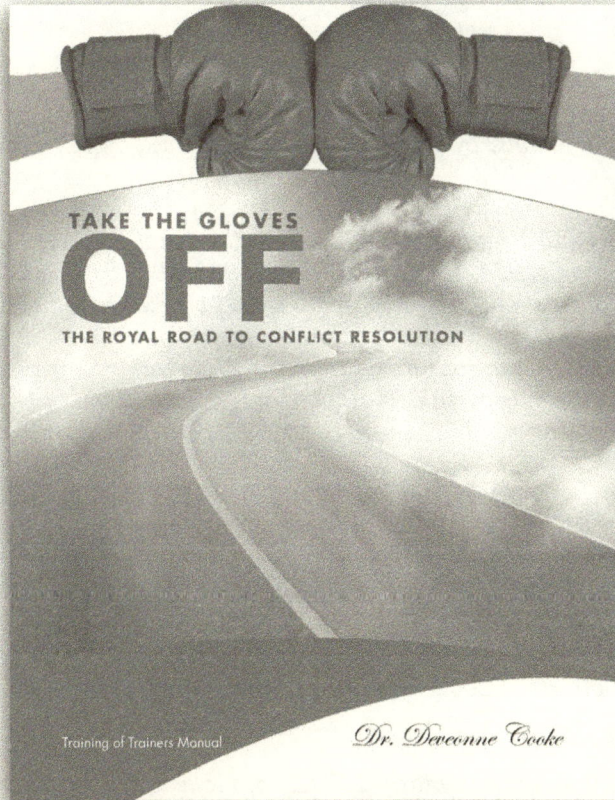

TAKE THE GLOVES
OFF
THE ROYAL ROAD TO CONFLICT RESOLUTION

Training of Trainers Manual

Dr. Deveonne Cooke

For more information, registration, to order resources or to book Dr. Cooke for speaking engagements, contact:

WISEWORD Publishing, LLC
1799 W. 5th Avenue, Suite 125
Columbus, Ohio 43212
Phone: 614-419-7189
E-mail: DrCooke@WISEWORD.us

Website: www.WISEWORD.us

Additional Copyright Information

Scripture marked (KJV) taken from the King James Version. Scripture taken from the New King James Version. Copyright © 1982 by Thomas Nelson, Inc. Used by permission. All rights reserved.

Scripture quotations taken from the Amplified® Bible, Copyright © 1954, 1958, 1962, 1964, 1965, 1987 by The Lockman Foundation. Used by permission (www.lockman.org).

Scripture quotations taken from the 21st Century King James Version®, copyright © 1994. Used by permission of Deuel Enterprises, Inc., Gary, SD 57237. All rights reserved.

Scripture taken from the HOLY BIBLE, TODAY'S NEW INTERNATIONAL VERSION®. Copyright © 2001, 2005 by Biblica®. Used by permission of Biblica®. All rights reserved worldwide.

Scripture taken from The Message. Copyright © 1993, 1994, 1995, 1996, 2000, 2001, 2002. Used by permission of NavPress Publishing Group.

Scripture quotations marked (NLT) are taken from the Holy Bible, New Living Translation, copyright © 1996, 2004, 2007 by Tyndale House Foundation. Used by permission of Tyndale House Publishers, Inc., Carol Stream, Illinois 60188. All rights reserved.

Scripture taken from the NEW AMERICAN STANDARD BIBLE®, Copyright © 1960,1962,1963,1968,1971,1972,1973,1975,1977,1995 by The Lockman Foundation. Used by permission.

NOTES:

www.ingramcontent.com/pod-product-compliance
Lightning Source LLC
LaVergne TN
LVHW041206080426
835508LV00008B/826